Powhatan Bouldin

The Old Trunk

Sketches of Colonial Days

Powhatan Bouldin

The Old Trunk
Sketches of Colonial Days

ISBN/EAN: 9783337155247

Printed in Europe, USA, Canada, Australia, Japan

Cover: Foto ©ninafisch / pixelio.de

More available books at **www.hansebooks.com**

—OR—

SKETCHES OF COLONIAL DAYS.

—BY—

POWHATAN BOULDIN,

AUTHOR OF

HOME REMINISCENCES OF JOHN RANDOLPH.

··

RICHMOND, VA.:

ANDREWS, BAPTIST & CLEMMITT, STEAM PRINTERS.

1888.

THE OLD TRUNK.

CHAPTER I.

THE FRONTIER OF HALIFAX THREATENED—ORDER TO MARCH—
SKETCHES OF CLEMENT READ, THOMAS BOULDIN AND ABRA-
HAM MAURY.

I had an aunt who lived to be ninety-four years of age;
her mother was ninety-three. My aunt was the grand-
daughter of one of the first settlers of Charlotte county,
Va. That old pioneer kept his important papers in a
trunk, and a very ancient piece of workmanship it was.
It was a trunk when the timbers of the oldest houses in
the country were growing in the forest, and when the
richest lands were sold for a trifle. It performed its
daily office when there was a vice-royal court at Williamsburg, whence our ancestors received their commissions under the hands of the Colonial Governors of Virginia. To its safe-keeping valuable papers were en-
trusted when the church wardens contracted for the
building of the first church in the county. It has sur-
vived the ruins of the first settlements made by the white
man; it received the last curse of the red man, as he
stood over the graves of his forefathers, and caught the
last echo as he retreated toward the setting sun: it saw
the parting look which he cast upon his hunting grounds,
and the scowl upon his countenance as he heard the
forests resound with the axes of the white men.

This depository of memorials of the past was handed down
from father to son, and twenty-four years ago my aunt

4

went to it, and taking out a bundle of papers solemnly delivered them to me, having on former occasions, told me all about them and the men and things of the olden time. And, reader, if you have a curiosity to examine these papers with me, and would like to read sketches of some of the old pioneers of Charlotte, and get a glimpse of colonial life, I will open the Old Trunk for you; selecting only such documents as are of historic value.

Are you not curious to know what you will see, *first?* when it was written: by whom: and what it is about?

"April 18th, 1758.

"Capt. Bouldin:

"You, with the men under your command, are to march to Halifax Court-house, there to joyn a company raised by Col. Maury, whose orders you are to receive.

"I am informed that Major Harris has received costs and orders from the government to furnish such forces as are sent to the assistance of Halifax county with provisions. To Col. Maury then you are to apply for his orders to Major Harris for a supply for your men. In the meantime you are to take the steps appointed by law to procure those necessary.

"Col. Maury will meet you at the Court-house, and give you directions where to march to the relief of the frontier of this county.

"I am, your humble servant,

Clem't Read."

"P. S.—You must cause your Lieutenant to keep an exact journal of all your marches, and the different routes you take, and of all transactions relating thereto, that it may be returned to the President at Williamsburg, according to order.

"You must also cause him to keep an exact muster-roll, and keep an account of all provisions expended on the company, and of all the ammunition, &c.

C. R."

5

Before I proceed to comment upon the foregoing military order, I will lay before the reader another little slip, written seven months later. It is as follows:

"LUNENBURG COUNTY, &c.,
November Court, 1758.

There was levied by the Court the sum of fifty pounds, current money, to be collected by the Sheriff and paid to Thomas Bouldin, Gent., for him to purchase armes for the poor, &c., according to Act of Assembly.

CLEMENT READ, C. L. C."

The foregoing documents carry us back 18 years before the Revolution, to the time when the French and Indian war was in progress, when Francis Fauquier was Governor of the Colony, before Charlotte county was cut off from Lunenburg, when the Indian still lingered around the graves of his forefathers, and wild beasts roamed the forests of the valleys of the Staunton and the Dan.

Three old stocks, Read, Bouldin and Maury, are mentioned, from whom have sprung numerous descendants.

Clement Read is the ancestor of all the Reads that the writer knows anything about, and his descendants, like the descendants of Col. Bouldin, are scattered all over the United States. He was the old clerk of Lunenburg, and the father of Col. Thomas Read, the first clerk of Charlotte; the grandfather of the late Rev. Clement Read, who lived on Staunton river, and the great-great-maternal grandfather of the writer.

The first that is known of him is his landing at Williamsburg, being a small lad. Where he originally came from I do not know. Being a sprightly and prepossessing youth, Speaker Robinson took a fancy to him, and sent him to William and Mary College, where he graduated. He afterwards went to King and Queen county, where he married a wealthy and most accomplished lady, whose maiden name was Mary Hill. She lived at "White

Bank," the old Robinson homestead, and it was there that Clement Read, the adopted son of John, or "Speaker" Robinson, first saw her. The house in which she lived, and in which she was married, is still standing, and it is said to be one of the oldest houses in that section of country.

Clement Read settled in Lunenburg (now Charlotte) in the year 1733. His residence was on Roanoke, about two and a-half miles from the present county seat, which was named Marysville, in honor of his wife; it has since been changed to Smithville. Col. Read owned not less than 100 slaves, and lived in elegant style. Wealthy, highly educated, possessed of a fine understanding and captivating manners, he wielded great influence in the Colony. He built the first framed house which was built in Charlotte. All the country around Danville was in forest at that time, inhabited by wild beasts—bears, wild cats and buffaloes. This fact is ascertained from Byrd's account of his journey to his "Land of Eden" in 1733. That was the name which he gave to the twenty thousand acres of land which he took up as compensation for his services for running the dividing line between Virginia and North Carolina. The Indians had not left the country: for, on one occasion, he says, his surveying party were alarmed by a report of one of his woodsmen, who stated that he had followed the track of a great body of Indians to the place where they had lately encamped. Col. Byrd quieted them as well as he could, by telling them, "if they were Catawbas there was no danger, because they were too fond of our trade to lose it for the pleasure of shedding a little English blood." He describes the beautiful spot (above Danville) where the Sauro Indians once lived, but who were driven south by the frequent inroads of the Senecas.

The "Land of Eden" passed from the Byrds into the hands of a man by the name of Farley. The tradition which we get from Mr. Geo. L. Aiken is, that Farley won the whole 20,000 acres of Col. Byrd at dice. Gen. Izzard, who married Farley's daughter, once lived in a small log house, which he built on the road from Danville to Cascade, just below Cascade creek. He sold most of the land after it had been divided into 16 parts. Patrick Henry once owned two of them, comprising between 2,000 and 3,000 acres. He gave them to his sons, Spotswood and Nathaniel. Mr. G. Winston, their brother-in-law, afterwards bought them, and sold them to various persons. The last remnant of Byrd's land (530 acres) was sold by Capt. Noble, of Danville, as attorney for a gentleman in Philadelphia, to Peter Scales, at the price of one dollar per acre.

At the time that Col. Byrd visited his "Land of Eden," and at the time that Col. Read moved to Charlotte, the settlers in Virginia, including the negroes, did not number 200,000; but there were many Indians, who were remnants of the thirty tribes between tide-water and the mountains, united in a grand confederacy under King Powhatan.

It appears from the foregoing order to march, that twenty-five years after Clement Read settled in Lunenburg, on the banks of the Little Roanoke, and twenty-five years after Col. Byrd made his journey to his "Land of Eden," on the banks of the Dan, the frontier of Halifax county was threatened. Halifax, at that time, included Pittsylvania, Patrick and Henry, and stretched far across the mountains.

The Bouldin, to whom the foregoing order was given, emigrated from Maryland to Lunenburg (now Charlotte) county in 1744. He was originally from the State of Pennsylvania. His father was an Englishman. His given

name was Thomas, and he built the second framed house that was built in Charlotte. He was a merchant and farmer at the same time, and at different times sheriff, magistrate and colonel of the militia. He was, besides, a most active and zealous member of the established Church. Business was his *forte*, and the most distinctive trait of his character was his great moral and physical courage. He died in 1783, having lived in his adopted county thirty-nine years. In the Old Trunk was found a copy of his will, made out by Thomas Read, clerk, from which it appears that he was a large land-holder. Among other tracts of land disposed of, I notice one of 760 acres in Henry county, given to his son Joseph. He was buried by the side of his wife, at the old homestead, which has been in the family one hundred and forty-eight years. He was the father of Major Wood Bouldin, an officer of the Revolution, the grandfather of Hons. Thos. T., James W. and Louis C. Bouldin, great grandfather of the late Judge Wood Bouldin, of the Supreme Court of Appeals of Virginia, and the ancestor of many bearing his name now residing in various parts of the United States.

The Maury, to whom Captain Bouldin was ordered to report, was Abraham Maury, son of Mathew Maury, who was born in Dublin, but died in Virginia in 1752. His wife's name was Mary Ann Fontaine. Abraham Maury married Susanna Poindexter and has a number of descendents in Virginia. The Rev. James Maury was a brother of Abraham, and the great-grandfather of the distinguished Commodore Mathew Fontaine Maury, whose fame extends over the civilized world. In a letter written in 1759, the Rev. James Maury, referring to Abraham Maury, says:

"My brother is concerned in victualizing the troops stationed on the southwestern frontier of this colony, and by his prudence, activity and spirited conduct, has

9

greatly contributed to keep the remote inhabitants from abandoning their habitations, and thereby has done no small service to his country."

How interesting the journal of the march of Captain Bouldin's and Colonel Maury's men would be if we had it, but history gives us no account of it. In fact, we find very little in history relating to Virginia in colonial days. The foregoing little slip of paper is all that we have to inform us that such an expedition was ever planned.

We are not surprised to find that the first script which we drew from the Old Trunk should introduce us to those old pioneers, Maury, Read and Bouldin, with swords in hand. Those times required all the nerve that is ever given to man. The whites were few, the savages numerous; cut off from the more settled parts of the colony by a vast trackless forest, our forefathers had to rely upon their own strong arms.

As we muse over this manuscript, its signature, its date, its unmistakable marks of age, we are carried back in imagination to those early times, and indulge our fancy until we hear the howling of the wolves before our doors and see the form of an Indian in pursuit of his prey.

CHAPTER II

Col. Bouldin's wife's maiden name was Nancy Clarke, and she brought with her, all the way from Maryland, a slip of her favorite (Damask) rose, which now (after the lapse of 144 years) blossoms and blooms on the old place belonging to Judge Thomas T. Bouldin, one of her descendants. She had to go at first into a log cabin, and when she entered it, finding no place to hang her gold lace hat, she *wept*.

On her way to her new home she came down the Chesapeake bay, and while on board of the vessel, she gave birth to a son. She travelled upwards of a hundred miles, in a wagon, through the country, thus passing through many rough and trying scenes; but her stout heart never gave way, until she entered her log cabin, to find no place for her gold lace hat. Then, it was that, for the first time, she *wept*.

The old pioneer knew that the tears which his wife shed on that occasion, were not the unmeaning drops that fall from a cloud of momentary disappointment; they spoke volumes, and he soothed her pain by promising her as comfortable a dwelling as the one she left in Maryland, and going to work in earnest, he soon redeemed his promise. He not only did that, but he was exceedingly active in destroying the savage features of their new home by the introduction of the arts of civilized life.

The house which he built was standing until after the war between the States. The writer remembers it well.

The most remarkable feature about it was the large fire place; a person five feet high might have stood up inside of it. No one ever looked at it, we venture to say, without being entirely satisfied that when it was built there was no scarcity of wood.

Col. Bouldin promised that when his new home was finished he would give a house-warming, and, true to his promise, when the last nail was driven he invited all his friends, far and near, to come. An advertisement was stuck up on the old Keysville road, in which were these words : " All are welcome who choose to come." an expression of a soul both large and free.

As might have been expected from such an universal invitation, preparations were made on a most extensive scale. A large ox was roasted whole; cider was sitting round, not in barrels but in hogsheads. Nor did our forefathers confine themselves to thin potations : they had rum, and it was not handed round in any of your small-sized bottles, but that, too, was in a hogshead already mixed into punch. All night and all the next day they danced and joked and frolicked to their heart's content.

Natural enough, one of the party got drunk, but Col. Bouldin, liberal as he was, was not the man to suffer his hospitalities to be abused, nor would he permit a drunken. turbulent fellow to disturb the festivities of this interesting occasion, so he tied him to a large oak tree in the back yard, and there he remained until the sun rose the next morning. The identical tree has been pointed out to me, and on account of this incident, I have looked at it with a very curious eye.

Some friendly Indians, who heard of the liberal terms of the invitation, came to join in the frolic and fun. Two

of them got drunk and became very obstreperous. The pioneer had them flogged until they were sober.

This circumstance of the manner in which he conducted himself at the house-warming, though trivial in itself, throws more light upon the character of this old first settler than pages of personified qualities.

I must not omit the dark features which form the background to the picture. There were at this frolic, in the capacity of servants, negroes fresh from Africa—"new negroes," as they were called. Such a curiosity has not been seen in Virginia for many a day. Col. Bouldin owned a large number of slaves, most of them "new negroes." "Daddy Will" was one of that class, and he had, what was rare with them, a *nose*. Most of them had only two holes to breathe through. "Daddy Will" represented himself to be the son of a King in his own country: he said he was taken prisoner of war in his own country: that the choice was given him, whether he should be sold into slavery or suffer death: that he preferred to be sold: was sold and transported to Virginia. Nor did he complain of his fate: he seemed to think it was all right. "But," said he to his master, "you must feed me: I fed my slaves when I had them." He had the carriage of a lofty conceit of grandeur, particularly when he put on his Sunday clothes. He would mount up in a large chair, which he made for himself, assuming airs of great dignity and consequence. If any one chanced to take his royal seat, it offended him highly. On such occasions he would say, "if you want to look grand you must make a chair of your own."

"Jack," was another "new negro." There was one thing remarkable about him—he fasted regularly on Fridays; nor could he be persuaded not to observe that religious rite. No one knew how he received his religious

impression. Perhaps it was from some zealous Catholic missionary.

There was a great difference between the negroes of different tribes; some were cannibals, while others were not. It was with some difficulty that the former could be kept from eating children, even under the eyes of the white people. Sometimes, as they would pass by a young fat baby, they would smack their mouths in savage zest for a morsel of human flesh.

Should this description of a house-warming fall into the hands of a descendant of the Puritans of New England, he would, in all probability, raise his eyes in holy horror at the idea of flogging an Indian; and especially would he be shocked if he were told that the "new negroes," who eat babies, had to be flogged, also, in order to be tamed. But, sons of Virginia sires, never do you mind what the descendants of the Puritans say. The old cavaliers did right. Men who had to deal with wild Indians and new negroes, could not afford to indulge in a sickly philanthropy. They had to act according to circumstances, and what is proper at one time, and with one race, may not be so at another time, and with a different race.

See what the Southern whites have done for the Africans brought here, for the most part in Northern vessels! How different is the negro of the present day from a native African? And yet the old slaveholder is blamed for the past. He gets no credit, in certain quarters, for having tamed the "new negroes," nor for having Christianized and civilized them.

I will now submit to the inspection of the inquisitive reader, a very suggestive little piece of paper:

"*Sir*,—You are to pay out of the depositum to Major Bouldin, the builder of Rough Creek church, the sum of sixty pounds, on his finishing the same. It has been viewed and approved of, and can't need a vestry to direct the same.

Therefore, please pay him that sum, and this shall be your indemnity at making up your accounts with the vestry.

Yours, &c.,

PAUL CARRINGTON,
C. READ,
C. Wardens.

To Mr. Jas. Speed, Collector of Cornwall Parish, October 17, 1769."

It thus appears that Thos. Bouldin built the first church, where the Rough Creek church now stands, and Paul Carrington and Clem't Read were officers.

The Church of England had been established from the beginning in Virginia. As fast as the country became settled, it was laid off in parishes, and every parish had a parson, who was furnished with a glebe and house, and his salary was raised by a levy of taxes upon all the inhabitants. There were four churches in Charlotte county, namely: Sandy Creek, Rough Creek, Roanoke and Ash Camp. At the time that the foregoing order was written, the dissenters were quite numerous and very active. Twenty years before, Governor Gooch made a speech to the grand jury of the general court in opposition to the Presbyterians, Methodists, and other denominations of Christians who were gaining ground in Virginia. Many ministers of the establishment had been forced to abandon their churches in Charlotte, which greatly disturbed these zealous old churchmen, Col. Read and Col. Bouldin, who held frequent consultations as to what was best to be done. One day Col. Bouldin remarked to Col. Read: "I know a man who can stand them (the dissenters), Parson Johnston is the man."

They were determined old men. They loved their Church. This was perhaps the strongest sentiment in their breasts, and they had no idea of giving it up without a struggle. It was agreed to send for Parson Johnston.

Col. Bouldin had known him in Maryland before he emigrated to Charlotte, and he could vouch for his ability and fitness. So he hitched up two four-horse wagons, his son driving one and old Harry, a colored man, the other, and started to Maryland.

After a long and toilsome journey of many hundred miles over the rugged roads of a new country, the wagons returned and landed the parson, his wife and children in Col. Bouldin's yard. A picture of the old parson and his family getting out of a four-horse wagon, and of their baggage wagon, containing everything they brought with them, would be highly interesting to us of our day.

Few men of any church have given more ample testimony of their zeal and fidelity to the cause.

The old parson had some stout work with the dissenters, but, we are informed, that he "stood them." He said: "I know when I have a good parish, if they don't know when they have a good parson."

Parson Johnston remained at his post a long time. He fought a good fight, but at last was forced to surrender to the overwhelming forces of the dissenters. He was doomed, moreover, to witness what was to him a heart-rending spectacle—some of his daughters captured by the dissenters. When he first heard of it, addressing himself to the son of the old pioneer, Col. Thos. Bouldin; " Wood," said he, " they have my child, and I expect they will get my wife." And the big tears rolled down his manly cheeks.

Paul Carrington, whose name is signed to the foregoing paper, went to Lunenburg (now Charlotte) a lad of sixteen or seventeen years. He was employed by Col. Read as deputy-clerk, but in a few years he began the practice of law, in which he was eminently successful. In the course of time he married a daughter of the old clerk, and we find him and his father-in-law working together

for the good of the established Church. Paul Carrington was a man of ability and learning, of great firmness and integrity. He was a distinguished citizen, and one whose memory the State of Virginia may proudly cherish. He filled many high positions in his day. For many years he was a member of the House of Burgesses; was a member of the Virginia Convention of 1776, and finally rose to a seat upon the Court of Appeals.

What a change has taken place since the old churchmen signed the foregoing order. The weather-beaten boards and the moss-covered shingles of the old church were removed, the foundation was undermined, and the whole fabric was brought to ruins, and upon its ruins was erected a new structure. The old glebe land was sold, and after a long and obstinate resistance, the old parson was deprived of his living and a new order of things was established. A stream of religious liberty was rising, and it rose higher and higher, until it swept every vestige of the old establishment away, and ended in perfect religious freedom.

CHAPTER III.

The following old commission, signed by Fran. Fauquier, may be a matter of curiosity to the reader:

"Francis Fauquier, Esq., His Majesty's Lieutenant-Governor and Commander-in-chief of the Colony and Dominion of Virginia,

"To Thomas Bouldin, Esq.:

By virtue of the power and authority to me given, as Commander-in-chief of the Colony, I do hereby constitute and appoint you, the said Thomas Bouldin, to be sheriff of the county of Lunenburg, during pleasure; and that you be accordingly sworn as soon as conveniently may be; and before you are sworn or admitted into the said office, you are to enter into bond before His Majesty's justices of the said county, with two or more good and sufficient sureties, in the sum of one thousand pounds, current money, to render to the auditor and receiver-general of His Majesty's revenue; a particular, perfect, and true account of His Majesty's rents and dues, arising within the said county, unto the several persons to whom the same shall be due and payable; and true performance to make of all matters and things relating to your office during your continuance therein. And I hereby command all His Majesty's subjects inhabiting the said county, and others actually there, to be aiding and assisting you, the said Thos. Bouldin, as sheriff of the county aforesaid, in all things belonging to your office of sheriff.

"Given under my hand and seal of the Colony, at *Williamsburg*, the seventh day of July, in the thirty-third year of His Majesty's reign, *Anno que Domini* 1759.

FRAN. FAUQUIER."

Among the old papers is found the following marriage certificate, which is in striking contrast with the marriage certificate of modern times:

LUNENBURG COUNTY, viz.:

Whereas there is a marriage suddenly intended to be solemnized between Elisha Faris and Mary Vaughn (spinster), of the county aforesaid, I do hereby certify that Thomas Vaughn, father of the said Mary, signify'd his consent to the said intended marriage, and, at the same time, the said Elisha Faris, with Jno. Vaughn, his security, entered into bond, in my office, in fifty pounds, current money, payable to the King, with condition that there is no lawful cause to obstruct the said marriage.

Given under my hand this first day of April. 1765.

SAM COBBS.

"To James Hunt, Gent., first justice in the commission of the peace of the county aforesaid."

Let us put our hands again into the Old Trunk and see what valuable memento of the past we shall draw next.

December 12, 1766.

Pay to Mr. Thomas Bouldin two hundred pounds of tobacco, and charge the same to Your ob't servant.

SAM'L COBBS.

To Mr. Nath. Hunt.

This brings to our minds a portion of the early history of Virginia, when the gardens and public squares of Williamsburg were planted in tobacco. "The weed" which has since become so popular in every quarter of the globe, was first discovered in America, and carried into Europe by Sir Francis Drake, about the year 1560, and Sir Walter Raleigh is said to have been the first Englishman who learned to smoke. It is related of him, that one day, while he was smoking in his room the servant girl came in, and seeing the smoke coming out of his mouth and nose, she took it into her head that he was on fire and dashed a whole pitcher of water upon him.

Col. Byrd, in his history of the dividing line, relates the following:

"These first adventurers made a very profitable voyage, raising at least a thousand per cent upon their cargo. Amongst other Indian commodities, they brought over some of that bewitching vegetable, tobacco, and this being the first that ever came to England, Sir Walter thought he could do no less than make a present of some of the brightest of it to his royal mistress for her own smoking. The queen graciously accepted of it, but finding her stomach sicken after two or three whiffs, it was presently whispered by the Earl of Leicester faction that Sir Walter had certainly poisoned her. But. her majesty soon recovering her disorder, obliged the Countess of Nottingham and all her maids to smoke a whole pipe out amongst them."

It was after the unsuccessful effort to make money by the exportation of soap, ashes and tar, that our forefathers commenced the cultivation of tobacco. In a short time it became the object of almost universal desire and it was used to a great extent as the circulating medium of the Colony, which fact explains the above order for two hundred pounds of that precious article.

At the time that the above order was given, tobacco was made from James river as far back as the settlements extended. It was put up in hogsheads and *rolled* from the farms to deep water, where the English vessels received it. One of the shipping places was at a landing now known as Claremont, which is midway between Norfolk and Richmond.

How rapidly the cultivation and use of tobacco has spread over the world since it was first discovered in America. The area cultivated in the United States in 1886 is put at 752,720 acres, yielding 562,736,000 pounds, valued at $43,265,568.

There was no such thing as a manufactory of tobacco in this country in 1766. Now the value of manufactured tobacco in the United States is estimated at $117,000,000. The annual product of the world is 1,200,000,000 pounds.

But how came the little piece of paper, which forms my text, to be preserved? We will place it back among its ancient companions. Perhaps, and at some future time, long after the writer has crossed the shadowy sea, some curious inquirer into the past may dive down deep beneath the records of later years to the bottom of the Old Trunk and resurrect it again.

Here is another little piece of paper which was preserved in the Old Trunk:

"ADVERTISEMENT.

"At Charlotte Court-house, on Saturday, the 12th this month, will be let to the lowest bidder, the maintenance for 12 months of Susanna Philby, William Gothard, —— Monday and Jno. Upcott, poor persons in the parish of Cornwall. By order of the Vestry.

CLEM'T READ,
P. CARRINGTON,
Ch. Ws.

December 7, 1767."

The above advertisement is a very suggestive memorial of the past. Poor persons put up to the lowest bidder! Hard lot indeed! No such proceedings in Virginia now, "By order of the Vestry." That reminds us of the old established Church. No such power is vested in the church of to-day. All that has passed away.

Eighteen years after the foregoing advertisement was posted up, an act was passed establishing perfect religious freedom, which crushed the Church of our forefathers, and never afterwards were the poor people of the parish put up at auction to the lowest bidder.

But who were those "poor persons of the parish of Cornwall?" Alas! They are forgotten. It is to be hoped that when they "shuffled off this mortal coil," they entered upon a brighter and happier career: for, in this world, they seemed to have drunk the very dregs of life.

CHAPTER IV.

LORD DUNMORE—THE OLD DOMINION—THE CAVALIERS.

Let us put our hands again into the Old Trunk, and see what other memento of the past it contains.

Here is a slip of paper upon which is printed in large type the following:

"John, Earl of Dunmore; Viscount Fincastle; Baron Murray of Blair, of Moulin and of Tillmet; Lieutenant and Governor-General of his Majesty's Colony and Dominion of Virginia, and Vice-Admiral of the same,

"To THOMAS BOULDIN, Esq.:

" By virtue of the power and authority to me given, as his Majesty's Lieutenant and Governor-General and Commander-in-chief in and over this Colony and Dominion of Virginia, with full power and authority to appoint all officers, both civil and military, within the same, I, reposing especial trust in your loyalty, courage, and good conduct, do, by these presents, appoint you, the said Thomas Bouldin, Lieutenant-Colonel of the militia of Charlotte, whereof Paul Carrington, Esq., is Lieutenant and Chief-commander: You are, therefore, to act as Lieut.-Colonel, by duly exercising the officers and soldiers under your command, taking particular care that they be provided with arms and ammunition, as the laws of the Colony direct: and you are to observe and follow such orders and directions, from time to time, as you shall receive from me, or any other of your superior officers, according to the rules and discipline of war, in pursuance of the trust reposed in you.

"Given at Williamsburg, under my hand and the seal of the Colony this 10th day of April, and in the —— year of his Majesty's reign, *Annoque Domini* 1773.

DUNMORE."

How does this long array of titles sound in Republican ears? How does it contrast with William Smith, Governor of Virginia?

Dunmore was the last of the Colonial Governors. Every one remembers how he removed the gunpowder from the magazine at Williamsburg to a man-of-war anchored off Yorktown—how the people of Williamsburg flew to arms and came near seizing the person of the governor himself. When he put his name to the foregoing commission he had only been in the Colony one year.

The post of Governor of the Colony of Virginia, was, at that time, by no means free from difficulties. Dunmore found this out as soon as he arrived. The very first legislature that met gave him a severe lecture on his disregard of the laws which protect the liberty of the citizen. Virginia had become an almost independent State.

There had been a long and bitter contest between the colonists and the mother country. In Virginia it was not a struggle for a change of the form of government. They did not quarrel because they were living under a monarchy. Unlike the settlers of the New England States, they cherished the laws of old England, and loved the constitution of the mother country. After the death of King Charles I., and the installation of Oliver Cromwall as Protector, the Colony of Virginia refused to acknowledge his authority. During the whole struggle between Charles I. and the Parliament, the Virginians were firm on the side of their king. After the king was beheaded, they acknowledged the authority of the fugitive prince, and actually continued the provisional government, under a commission which he sent to Sir William Berkeley from his retreat at Breda, and it is a well-established fact that Charles II. was proclaimed king in Virginia before he was in England. The fidelity of Virginia to the crown, it has been said, gave her the honored title of the "Old Dominion." But

Virginia, from its settlement, was termed Old Virginia, and soon, Old Dominion, certainly before the reign of Charles II.

The first settlers of the "Old Dominion" were Cavalier-English. Their commerce was direct with England. The Church of England was endeared to them by a thousand memories which could never be effaced. Their forefathers had fought and died for it. They felt for its usages the tenderest regard, and introduced into this wilderness the forms of their beloved establishment. The youth were educated by teachers brought from the mother country. All the habits and customs of the early settlers of Virginia were Cavalier-English. They indulged in all the amusements, and it must be admitted, *vices*, too, of "Merrie England." But above all they were distinguished for their high sense of honor and chivalrous bearing. The old cavalier had his faults, but they were not the faults of the Puritans who settled New England. He was fond of horse racing and card playing, and, was perhaps too convivial in his habits, but no "Blue Laws" were enacted in Virginia.

We repeat, Virginia did not furnish an instance of a people trying to throw off a government because it no longer suited them, but of a people determined to do it, because the rights and privileges of the government were denied to them.

While Dunmore was Governor, affairs were brought to a crisis. He was forced to leave his royal palace, and take refuge on board a ship anchored off Yorktown. He refused upon invitation of the Assembly to return to his palace, or to sign bills of the utmost importance to the Colony, and refused to perform this branch of duty, unless the Assembly would hold their meetings under the guns of his ship. The Governor was therefore declared to have abdicated. Delegates were then appointed to

meet in Richmond to organize a provisional form of government and a plan of defence. Upon the committee of Safety, among many distinguished citizens of Virginia, was Paul Carrington, of Charlotte, the same who is mentioned in the foregoing document as chief commander of the militia of that county.

These reflections were suggested by reading the foregoing commission, signed by the last Colonial Governor of Virginia. It is a printed form, with blanks left for names of parties Dunmore writes a bold hand. His letters are as large as capitals.

This old document is so tattered and torn, and the ink so pale that it can scarcely be read, but we pore over it with the interest of the explorer in the Holy Land. Indeed the contents of the Old Trunk are mementoes of the past, which have been dug up, as it were, from the stream of dumb forgetfulness; and fortune has been as capricious in her dealings with them as she is with individuals. Now, we draw from the Old Trunk a paper so dimmed by age as to be scarcely legible; presently we come across another of greater antiquity, with every word as plain as when it was written. So, to-day, we meet with a young man whose frame has been wrecked upon the shoals of time; to-morrow with an old man who retains the vigor and buoyancy of youth. Here is a female just verging upon womanhood, from whose cheeks the rose has faded and gone; there is another, the mother of a numerous offspring, who is beautiful to the last.

CHAPTER V.

Who is there that, if he came across a very old bundle of papers, would not feel some curiosity to look over them, and see who wrote them, how they were written, and what they were about? In the bundle before me, handed down from generation to generation, containing a variety of letters and documents relating to men and things of colonial days, we find many mementos which suggest interesting reflections; but its contents should be read when the bustle and business of the day are over, in the quiet night, when the imagination is at liberty to roam at large over the regions of the past.

We have before us a letter, written in a beautiful, small hand, one hundred and eleven years ago. It reads as follows:

"PETERSBURG, 15th May, 1777.

"SIR :

"Doct. Clark, at your request, has made inquiry of me about the sloop Swallow. She has come in, but brought no cargo of any value. A great part of her cargo—tobo.—remained unsold. However, I have procured you some salt (6 bushels), which you may have on application. I informed you when I was up Xmas that I had sold my part of the vessel and cargo before she went out, and you told me you did not want the money for your 2 hhds. I therefore procured 2 hhds. of equal weight for you, the notes of which you may have when you please.

Pray send me the money for, and on account of, the quantity of iron you have sold for me, after deducting a reasonable allowance for your trouble in selling it.

I am, sir,

Your mo. ob. serv't,

CHR. McCONNICO."

This letter is directed to "Col. Thomas Bouldin, in Charlotte, by Doct. Wm. Clark."

The next is a letter one hundred and twenty-seven years old:

GLASGOW, 12th Sept., 1761.

"SIR:

"This will be delivered you by Capt. Sinclair, of our ship Friendship, whom we have directed to load in James river to our address, and shall be much obliged by your assistance towards his dispatch. We propose to be fixed in London a few weeks hence, where we shall be ready to render you any service in our power, and do our utmost for your interest, either in the sale of what you may be pleased to consign us or in purchasing the goods you order, or any other transaction you entrust to our care. Should the tobacco you ship prove of good quality and come early to market, we make no doubt, from the present scarcity of good tobacco in London, but we shall be able to render satisfactory accounts, and as we propose (if we find proper encouragement) to have a ship in your river every spring and fall, you may depend on having your goods ship' you punctually twice a year, and delivered at such landing as you shall direct. We have often observed tobacco of good quality much injured by pressing, owing to its being packed in too high case, which we could wish our friends would avoid, as it renders it utterly unfit for any manufacturer in Britain.

You'll please give your orders in time for what insurance you would choose made on your tobacco and with the order for your goods, which we shall punctually comply with, and are, with sincere regards, sirs,

Your very ob't servants,

HUGH MILLER & Co."

The letter is addressed on the back "To Thomas Bouldin, Lunenburg county, Virginia, to the care of W. H. Wade." This paper is unruled and sealed with the old-fashioned red wafer. Envelopes were not in use at the time.

We are reminded by these letters of how commerce was conducted in those days. While New England had vessels of her own and was trading in all parts of the world, the Virginia colonists paid but little attention to commerce. The foregoing letter represents an English ship in the James and its captain getting up a cargo of freight. The vessel was to transport the tobacco across the waters and bring back everything needed in the colony—every article of comfort or luxury, besides preachers, teachers, books and blooded horses. Again, unlike the inhabitants of New England, they called Old England their *home*. And as the churchman brought with him the habits, feelings and sentiments of the Cavalier, so the early settlers of New England brought with them the tone of the Puritan. There were instances of the former going directly to the North, but a great majority of those who emigrated to America came to Virginia.

The fact that the Cavaliers settled Virginia and the descendants of the Puritans settled New England, accounts in a measure for the difference between a Virginian and a New Englander of the present day.

"Hugh Miller & Co.!" Can the oldest inhabitant tell anything about that old Scotch firm which did business in Glasgow and had customers in Lunenburg?

And who was W. H. Wade? Where are his descendants? Alas! in this wide world, they may be scattered over a dozen States and all be as ignorant of the graves of their ancestors as the remnant of the tribe of Sauro Indians are of theirs who sleep upon the banks of the Dan.

The Capt. Sinclair mentioned in the letter, or it may be a son of his, settled on James river near the present town of Claremont, and all the family of that name, no doubt, are derived from him. Capt. Arthur Sinclair, of the United States Navy, who died in Norfolk, doubtless was one of them. He distinguished himself in the war of 1812 by his gallantry, and married a Miss Kennon, mother of the late Col. Erasmus Kennon, of Mecklenburg county, Va., and mother of Mr. Arthur Sinclair, who became commodore in the United States Navy before he died. Commodore Sinclair left two daughters—one of whom was married to Dr. Conway Whittle; the other to Mr. Wm. C. Whittle, a captain in the United States Navy and commodore in the Confederate States Navy.

CHAPTER VI.

A REFUGEE TO CHARLOTTE FROM THE LOWER COUNTRY IN
1773.—A MIXED SCHOOL BROKEN UP—INTERESTING ANEC-
DOTES AND INCIDENTS OF COLONIAL TIMES.

I have previously stated that my grandmother lived to
be ninety-three years of age, and as it was from her that
my aunt received many of the traditions which she handed
down to me, I will give my readers a short fragment of
her history.

Her given name was Joanna, and she was the daughter
of John Tyler, of Williamsburg, and aunt of Ex-President
Tyler. After the death of her father, the war of the Revolution having been brewing for some time, she came to
Charlotte, as a refugee from the lower country, to remain
with her brother, Louis Tyler, who then resided at Red
Hill, where Patrick Henry is buried. That beautiful and
valuable place is now owned by Mr. W. W. Henry, the
grandson of the great orator of the Revolution. Louis
Tyler went in person to Williamsburg for his sister, and,
being a lawyer in full practice, he made extra exertions to
be at Charlotte Court. When he arrived at the village he
placed his sister at the tavern while he was engaged in
transacting his business in the court-house.

As soon as the young lady made her appearance, the
enquiry was made in the crowd, "Who is she?" and
"Where did she come from?"

"I don't know, but from Old Williamsburg, I suppose,"
responded Col. Thomas Bouldin.

31

Her polished manners and fashionable dress made him think so, for Williamsburg was at that time the seat of learning in the Colony, and rivaled the Court of St. James in refinement and fashion. The great parade which had been made over Lord Dunmore's arrival left an indelible impression upon the mind of Miss Tyler, and she entertained the ladies of her new acquaintance with some very agreeable gossip concerning the celebrated ball which was given to his lordship by the citizens of Williamsburg.

Just here, it may interest my readers to tell them of a great frost, which my grandmother said occurred the year she came to Charlotte. She said, that on the 4th day of May, 1773, her brother's family sat down to dinner with a fine dish of English peas on the table; but that it was the last for that season. It was distressing to the eye, she added, to see the vegetation all killed and withered by the untimely frost.

Her brother having died while the Revolution was in progress, she did not feel safe to return to the lower country, but accepted the invitation of Isaac Read, son of Clement Read, to spend the time at his hospitable house until the storm passed over. There she met with Maj. Wood Bouldin, who was then a recruiting officer, and was married to him, Parson Johnston performing the ceremony. In five days afterwards Maj. Bouldin left his bride for the war.

On the 15th day of January, 1845, Mrs. Joanna Bouldin departed this life. After remaining sixty-eight years on the same place, forty-five of which she was a widow, she was buried with her husband and his father and mother.

I have previously stated, that as my great-grandmother, the wife of the old pioneer, was coming down the Chesapeake Bay, on her way from Maryland to her new home,

she gave birth to a son. That son's name was Richard, and when the announcement of his birth was made, a shout went up from all the crew: "A soldier is born to his Majesty;" and wines and cordials were sent to cheer the heart of the heroic mother.

That son used wickedly to say: "By G—d! I was not born in any country—I was born on the *Chesapeake Bay.*" And in truth, he seemed to feel something of the lawless spirit of the Corsair upon his ocean home, unrestrained by the laws of any clime.

A characteristic anecdote is told of him, which we will repeat for the entertainment of the reader:

About ten years before the Revolution of 1776, in the county of Charlotte, in the vicinity of old Roanoke church, there was a certain school for white children, where a free negro was taught with the other scholars. The rising generation must bear in mind, that while those were days of slavery there were a few colored people who enjoyed many of the privileges of freedom. But then, as now, and ever will be, social equality was looked upon with horror.

Complaint that a negro boy was attending the above-mentioned school was made to Major Wood Bouldin.

"Never mind," said he, "Dick will put that matter straight."

Sure enough, one morning, Dick, without saying a word to anyone, blew his horn and his dogs answered to the call. Off he started to the school-house. When he arrived at his point of destination, he dismounted from his horse, his dogs following him, went into the school-room, took the obnoxious individual by the collar and precipitated him out of doors.

That school-master left for parts unknown.

Such was the feeling at that time against any approach toward negro equality. All the State laws were wisely

constructed so as to favor the pretensions of the white race to superiority and supremacy.

All the artificial props have been violently knocked from under the white man, we shall see if there be not a natural barrier to social equality, grounded in the nature of man, and more impregnable than the forts of Gibraltar.

Rummaging over the papers of the Old Trunk, I chanced to stumble over the name of Jos. Lankford, and turning to my interpreter, I inquired who was he. She told me that he settled at what is now known as Coles Ferry, on the Staunton, in Charlotte county, in 1771, and that he, to use an old English phrase, spent his fortune "like a gentleman and a man of honor."

An amusing anecdote is told of this old man of jovial habits of the olden time, which will no doubt interest some of my readers, and perchance it may strike a chain of association, waking up some long lost treasure.

Mr. Lankford, we are informed, built his house as he conceived, above high water mark, nor could all the persuasions of the experienced ferryman living at the place, induce him to select a sight one foot higher. Nothing which he was told of former high-water marks, made from time to time, could induce him to believe that the river would ever shake the firm foundations of his house. He turned a deaf ear to the warning voice of the experienced ferryman, and he did it to his sorrow.

He had not been at his new home many years before the Staunton, on a memorable occasion, began to roll down an angry volume of water from the melting snow on the surrounding hills and the mountains away beyond. It soon covered the river bottoms and began to inch upon the seconds, but Lankford enjoyed his peace of mind, and what was more, his punch. He sat in the door and took his drinks, and viewed without alarm the rising floods.

34

In this state of fancied security he remained, although he saw the water oozing through the cracks of the floor. The kind and thoughtful ferryman went promptly to the relief of the distressed family. He offered them a safe passage to shore in his little canoe, which they accepted and joyfully embarked for land. But the incredulous head of the family refused to go one step with his wife and children. In the meantime the swelling tide rose higher and higher. It went gushing through the doors and windows, sweeping everything before it. Among other things, hen houses were seen floating down the stream and the cocks crowing as they went along.

The ferryman again launched his canoe to remonstrate with the drowning man. This time he found him sitting in the up-stairs window mixing his punch with the water from the river.

"Well, Joe, are you ready to go now," inquired the kind hearted and patient ferryman?

"Yes," he replied; "I didn't know the d——d tricks of the river."

We warrant the old fellow never built afterwards where an experienced ferryman advised him not to.

The following little incident carries us back more than a hundred years, and conveys to our minds a lively picture of the state of religious feeling in colonial times:

While the people generally were preparing to throw off the British yoke, and with it the Established Church, there were some who never forsook the Church of their fore-fathers, and Mrs. Joanna Bouldin was one of them.

There was a wag in the neighborhood by the name of Jarrold Sullivant, who on one occasion attended a revival of religion conducted by the dissenters. The greatest excitement prevailed, and in the midst of it he jumped up, clapped his hands, and turning to his wife, exclaimed:

"I am a changed man; it hasn't been five minutes since I thought Mrs. Ward the d—st fool in the country."

"You see there what the Lord can do," said Mrs. Spencer (a zealous dissenter) to Mrs. Bouldin.

"And you'll see what Jarrold can do," was the tart reply.

It was generally believed that he took that method of saying what he really thought of Mrs. Ward.

I will now relate an incident which occurred at the residence of Louis Tyler, which throws some light upon the institutions of colonial times. Our ancestors had apprenticed white servants, as well as colored slaves, in those days. Some of them were criminals sent over to the Colony to expiate their crimes, but others were good honest people, who, having no means to pay for their passage over to America, were sold for that purpose to wealthy planters. Isaac Read, son of Col. Clement Read, bought two of these servants: Louis Tyler one, whose name was Milly Collins, an upright woman, and of great fidelity. Serving her time without a murmer, but anxiously awaiting the expiration of her term of bondage, she calculated the very hour when she was to be free.

One night, as Mrs. Tyler was preparing to retire to bed, she, as usual, requested Milly to pull off her stockings. "Everybody pulls off their own stockings to-night," was her reply.

Pretty bold for her! But the hour of her deliverance had come, and she meant to assert her right that very instant, and her independent spirit will be admired by all who may chance to read the pages of this little narrative.

The following anecdote comes to me through the same channel which conveyed to me all the traditions in the Old Trunk:

"Madam Read," as she was called, the widow of Col. Clement Read, was regular in calling up the family (black

and white) to prayers, and as she would read certain commandments from the book, "Old Betty Gall," a favorite colored servant, invariably seated herself by the coffee-pot. It was her business to nurse it, and to have it strong for breakfast. When her mistress got to this part, "Lord, have mercy on us, and incline our hearts to keep this law," she would repeat it, emphasizing "*this law*," and shaking the coffee-pot at the same time, as much as to say, *nursing the coffee-pot* was the law *she* had to keep.

I will close the chapter by relating what occurred during the last illness of Col. Read, the man whose name is seen upon so many papers in the Old Trunk, the old clerk of Lunenburg, the zealous old churchman. He was lying in bed, unable to get up. His wife had gone to dinner, leaving Mrs. Elliot, their daughter, to nurse him during the short space of time that she would be absent. His mind was on the disposition which he had made of his property, and he seemed to have repented of what he had done. He requested his daughter to go to the drawer and bring him a certain piece of paper, describing it. It was brought to him. He took it in his trembling hands and held it to his fading sight, and having satisfied himself that she had found the right one, he commanded her to commit it to the flames.

That paper was his last will and testament, and as the law of primogeniture prevailed at that time, his oldest son Clement inherited the whole estate, but, being too generous to take it all, he divided it equally among his brothers.

The merit of such men consists in having hearts easily impressed with liberal sentiments and minds which elevate them to the mountain top, where they catch the first rays of the rising sun. Public opinion was tending fast towards the abolition of entails and primogeniture.

37

Those laws would have been abolished if Jefferson had never lived, but not so soon. He had the capacity to see the coming light *first*—but in the course of time, the sun would have climbed the mountain and shown himself to all.

It is still in the power of every testator to leave his whole estate to his first born. The old feelings upon this subject have died out. Public sentiment has acted upon the laws, and the laws have in turn acted upon public sentiment, so that we scarcely ever hear of gross inequality in the distribution of any estate. But there are few old homesteads now, such as there were in colonial times, with traditions and sweet reminiscences clustering around them.

If the eldest son of Col. Read had held on to the old "Bushy Forest" homestead, and if the laws of primogeniture had prevailed to the present time, the descendants of the old forefather might be able to find his grave.

> " There on his sleep of death might friendship pause,
> Dwell on past days and leave him with a sigh."

It is well to have such feelings, they fill the soul with pleasing melancholy thoughts; they allay the tumult of our veins. But if such feelings can only be secured at the expense of natural right and justice, they had better be sacrificed. It is better not to be able to find the graves of our forefathers, if they can only be found by a visit to some first born, elevated above his brethren and taking to himself the whole substance of his father.

CHAPTER VII.

It is not generally known that, during the revolutionary
war which severed our connection with Great Britain,
there was an encampment of French soldiers in Charlotte
county, Va. They were stationed at the court-house, and
the headquarters of the officers was at Madam Read's—
" Bushy Forest," as it is now called.

On one occasion a deserter from the enemy, who had
been advertised and for whom a reward had been offered,
was brought in. When he was delivered up to the authorities the officer to whom he was delivered threw the
gold at the person who had made the arrest, saying:
" There is the price of blood."

Talking about the French Encampment brought to the
mind of our interpreter of the Old Trunk the only time
that the pious old pioneer of Charlotte, Col. Thomas
Bouldin, was ever known to swear.

Some commissary stores of our army were kept in a
building belonging to him. Hearing that the French
were breaking open his doors and throwing the goods into
the road in order to make comfortable quarters for the
soldiers, he went at once to see what was going on. He
passed a sentinel who said something to him in French;
but the old gentleman, remarking that he himself knew
nothing of the rules of war, passed on. A soldier with
his axe raised, was in the act of cutting down the door of
one of his houses. As he approached the soldier turned

around with his axe still elevated. Colonel B., supposing he meant to turn upon him, exclaimed: "Strike away, you d——d scoundrel, you can't rob me of many days."

He said: "It was enough to make a parson swear."

May not that oath be like Uncle Toby's? which was immediately carried up to heaven and blotted out by the tear of the recording angel as he wrote it down.

The French officers took a great fancy to Mrs. Joanna Bouldin, partly on account of her French extract and partly on account of her musical talent. They used frequently to go to hear her play on the spinet. She had the only one at that time in the county. It was before pianos were invented. This same old spinet is now in the possession of one of the members of the family, preserved as a sacred relic of the past. The writer remembers to have heard her play on it when *she* was very old and *he* was quite young.

Mrs. B. said the French kept up a mighty cooking over the opposite side of the road. One day they cooked up a quantity of muscles and brought her a dish. She informed them that nothing could induce her to eat one. They insisted, saying: "'Tis good, madam, 'tis good." But the politeness of Frenchmen even was not sufficient to overcome her natural prejudice.

She was on one occasion invited to headquarters to partake of an extra dinner given by the officers. Having accepted the invitation, at the appointed time she was present, and when dinner was announced she took her seat at the table. To her great horror she was asked to take a piece of an "American pullet, better known as the turkey buzzard." By a great effort of self-possession she managed to control her feelings long enough to get up from the table, complaining of being sick.

40

The French, we know, eat horses and cats, but we had not supposed they had the stomach for buzzards. It is said they prepared them for the table by burying them for some time in the ground.

The conduct of the French on the occasion referred to, in breaking open the houses which contained the commissary stores, gave offense to the county court. A letter of complaint was written and the sheriff directed to deliver it to the commanding officer. That official expressing some reluctance to go on such a mission, Major Wood Bouldin offered his services, which were accepted.

When the communication was delivered at headquarters, the statements contained in it were pronounced false.

"They are not false," responded Major B., and he was immediately arrested and a guard placed around the house, and the whole of Madam Read's family confined to one room.

Major B., said the interpreter, was running up and down stairs nearly all night, while he stood anxiously awaiting their decision. Just before the dawn of day they released him, when he rode home to the great relief of his wife.

The old people, in after times, used to love to talk of what happened at "Madam" Read's when the French officers were there.

I will close this chapter with what very few persons have ever seen—a patent for land granted 132 years ago. It is a valuable document to show the changes which have taken place in the laws of the land. The handwriting of the old colonial Governor who signed it is very distinct.

The following is a copy of the original deed:

"George the Second, by the Grace of God of Great Britain, France and Ireland, King Defender of the Faith, &c. To all to whom these presents shall come, greeting: Know ye that for divers good causes and considerations,

but more especially for and in consideration of the sum
of three pounds, of good and lawful money for our use,
paid to our Receiver-General of our Revenues, in this our
Colony and Dominion of Virginia—we have given, granted
and confirmed, and by these presents for us our heirs and
successors—do give, grant and confirm unto Thomas
Bouldin, one certain tract or parcel of land containing
nine hundred and seventy acres, lying, and being in the
county of Lunenburg. [Here follows a description of
the land, which we omit.]

With all woods, under-woods, swamps, marshes, low-
grounds, meadows, feedings, and his due share of all veins,
mines and quarries as well discovered as not discovered
within the bounds aforesaid, and being part of the said
quantity of nine hundred and seventy acres of land and
the rivers, waters and water courses therein contained,
together with the privileges of hunting, hawking, fishing,
fowling and all other profits, commodities and heredita-
ments, whatsoever to the same or any part thereof, belonging or in any wise appertaining to have, hold, possess
and enjoy the said tract or parcel of land, and all other
the before granted premises, and every part thereof, with
their and every of their appurtenances unto the said
Thomas Bouldin and to his heirs and assigns forever, to
the only use and behoof of him, the said Thomas Bouldin,
and to his heirs and assigns forever, to be held of us, our
heirs and successors as of our manor of East Greenwich,
in the county of Kent in free and common soccage, and
not in capite or by knights service yielding and paying
unto us, our heirs and successors, for every fifty acres of
land, and so proportionably for a lesser or greater quantity
than fifty acres, the fee rent of one shilling yearly, to be
paid upon the feast of St. Michael, the archangel, and also
cultivating and improving three acres, part of every fifty of
the tract above mentioned, within three years after the date
of these presents, excepting for so much of the said land
as hath been already cultivated and improved according
to the condition of the said former patent, provided always
that if three years of the said fee rent shall at any time
be in arrear and unpaid, or if the said Thomas Bouldin,
his heirs or assigns, do not within the space of three years

next coming after the date of these presents, cultivate and improve three acres, part of every fifty of the tract above mentioned, except as is before excepted; then the estate hereby granted shall cease and be utterly determined, and hereafter it shall and may be lawful and for us, our heirs and successors, to grant the same land and premises with the appurtenances unto such person or persons as we, our heirs and successors, shall think fit. In witness whereof, we have caused these, our letters patent to be made. Witness our trusty and well-beloved Robert Dinwiddie, Esq., our Lieutenant-Governor and Commander-in-Chief of our said Colony and Dominion at Williamsburg, under the seal of our said Colony, the sixteenth day of August, one thousand seven hundred and fifty-six, in the thirtieth year of our reign.

Robert Dinwiddie.

There was in the Old Trunk another patent, granted by George III, to Thomas Bouldin for four hundred and sixty acres of land, dated on the 10th day of July, 1767, and signed by " Fran. Fauquier." It is a printed form on parchment with space left for a description of the land to be made in writing, which is done in such a manner as to fill us with admiration for the penmanship of the scribe; and it was written with a quill pen, nor are there any lines to go by, although the parchment is more than three times as wide as the pages of this book. I wish I could show my readers the long lines so *straight* and so beautifully written. Now-a-days, we have steel pens and paper nicely ruled, but do we write any better than our forefathers? Judging from the specimens I see in the Old Trunk, I should say we do not write as well. Does it not seem to you reader, that the more you fix for a scribe, the less pains he takes?

The first thing, I dare say, which struck the reader when he read the foregoing document was the useless verbiage. A deed for the same land now, leaving out the description

as is done in this case, can be written in a dozen lines. The next thing is the price of the land—five pounds for nine hundred and seventy acres. Lastly, the conditions on which the grant was made.

Times change and nothing shows it plainer than the patent which I have copied for the inspection of the thoughtful reader.

CHAPTER VIII.

I will now make my last drawing from the Old Trunk. What, reader, do you suppose I have this time for your dissection and entertainment?—Two account books, 129 years old, which belonged to my great-grandfather.

The first is headed: "The Country Corn," and the accounts are neatly kept in a little home-made book, ruled by the old merchant himself, and on excellent paper, which bears the mark of having been made in England. The hand-writing is excellent, and every entry is as plain as it was when it was first made.

It appears that the authorities, away back in 1759, contracted with Thomas Bouldin to haul 89 barrels of corn from Petersburg, and deliver the same to various and sundry persons whose names are down in the book. The distributing point is not stated; but the presumption is that it was at "Bouldin's Store," on the old Keysville road, not far from Drake's Branch Depot.

James Walden's is the first name on the book; he received 2½ bushels of corn on the 16th day of May, 1759; Clement Read, Sen'r. received 2½ bushels on the 16th of May, and 3 barrels and 1 bushel on the 9th of June. He is the only man who seemed to have received as much as 3 barrels. One man got only a half a bushel. The first distribution took place in the middle of May, and the second in the middle of June.

45

At the end of the book is the following:

"1759.—The Country to Thos. Bouldin Dr.:
To bringing up two loads corn from point,
ten barrels each load, - - - £5
To 2½ barrels lent, that I never rec'd again, 1 17s. 6d.
To receiving and delivering 89 barrels, as
p'r acc't.

"LUNENB'G:
This day, Capt. Thos. Bouldin came before
me, Thos. Bedford, Gent., and made oath that the services
contained in this acct. in delivering and receiving the corn,
and the lent 2 barr'ls and a half, and bringing up two
loads from Petersburg to Lunenburg, were performed by
him, and that he never yet received any satisfaction for the
same.
Given under my hand this 12th April, 1764.
THOS. BEDFORD."

The old gentleman, whose signature is to the above
paper, was a valuable citizen in the Colony, and from him
has sprung a numerous and highly respected progeny.

But to return to the account-book. From the foregoing extract the reader may figure out the price of corn in
1759; also, the cost of transportation by wagon from
Petersburg. He will discover, too, that "Capt." Bouldin
was five years getting his pay, if he ever got it.

I find another little account-book, which furnishes food
for reflection. It is dated 1763.

In this Samuel Wimbish is charged to wagoning 2 hhds.
shells (oyster shells, doubtless, to make lime), and he had
to pay two pounds and three shillings for it. Joseph
Friend and Thomas Spencer are charged with hauling
merchandise. The Friends, the Wimbishes and the Spen-
cers, who are scattered all over the country at the present
time, are no doubt branches of those old honored stocks.

We find a very distinguished name in this old account-
book, namely: that of Paul Carrington. The reader can-

not guess what he is charged with—"Hauling fifteen gallons rum." Though a strict member of the Established Church and entirely sober in his habits, it seems that the "Old Virginia gentleman" was not a "teetotaller."

The people in those days drank rum. We don't find any whiskey on the accounts of the merchants of colonial times. Our forefathers who were fond of a glass of toddy, labored under one serious disadvantage—they had no ice. The first ice-house ever dug in the county, was on the place recently owned by Mr. Henry Carrington, deceased, but it was built long after the time of which we are writing.

The name of Paul Carrington appears in two places. The last charge made against him is, "To bringing three negroes up."

This was one hundred and twenty-nine years ago. They were brought up from Petersburg and no doubt were "new negroes."

Our forefathers found themselves in the midst of a wilderness of forest. They were greatly in need of labor. Here was a race of Aborigines right on the spot, infinitely inferior to themselves in many respects. And yet they derived no advantage from them in clearing the forests and cultivating the soil. The negro must be brought thousands of miles from his native land at great expense, and made to lend a helping hand towards the development of the resources of the country.

But why was the African enslaved and the Indian made to follow the course of the buffalo? It was not from any scruples of conscience entertained by the Cavalier of the South or the Puritan of New England, but simply because the red man of America had too fiery a nature to be subjugated.

While we do not justify the means used in emancipating the negro, we would not have him back in slavery again.

47

But who can reflect calmly and seriously upon his condition as he was, and now is, without admitting that the institution of slavery was, perhaps, the only means of enabling him to take the first step towards civilization.

I purpose now to publish the 120 names which are found in the book wherein the "Country Corn" was kept. Many of our readers will find the names of their ancestors in the list. Just here I take occasion to remark, that there is not a single middle name among them.

To show the difference in this respect, between these times and those, I took 120 names as I came to them on the subscription book of a newspaper now published in Danville, with the following result: Middle names, 108; names without a middle name, 12; now and then a parent gives his child four initials, such as L. Q. C. L. Such long names are an unnecessary tax upon our time and memories, and it is a great pity that we have departed from the example set us by our forefathers.

There is another fact disclosed by the papers in the "Old Trunk." It is this: Only one man, namely, Samuel Cobbs, Clerk of Charlotte in 1766, makes a display of his handwriting. His flourishes would do credit to a graduate of a modern business college. Nor does he confine the capers of his pen to his name, he curls all over his official papers. About ten years ago, my respected friend, James M. Whittle, Esq., of Pittsylvania county, Va., wrote some highly interesting memoirs of the late William Leigh, in which he complimented him for never, in all his writing, making a solitary unnecessary stroke of the pen. Flourishes are ostentatious, and interfere with reading. Surely, the best writing is that which can be most easily read. Will not every printer in the land say amen?

But I am digressing. Here are the names, copied *literatim:*

48

James Waldin,
Richard Crews,
John Crews,
Thos. Handcock, Sen'r,
Benjamin Handcock,
Wm. Addams, Sen'r,
John Smith,
George Foster, Jun'r,
Richard Jones,
John Stewart,
Martha Hill,
Charles Swillivant,
Francis Worsham,
William Tibbs,
Thomas Huddlestone,
Susannah Jones,
David Roberts,
Richard Hix, Jun'r,
Ann Harwood,
Wm. Nicholas,
Isaac Barnet,
Abraham Lunderman,
Wm. Toombs,
James Shelton,
Wm. Traynum,
Francis Petty,
Partrick Still,
Micajah Francis,
John Worthey,
Wm. Chandler,
Thomas Handcock, Jr.,
Thomas Comer,
John Nance,
Thomas Price,

Dan'l Slayton,
Arthur Slayton,
Zachariah Waller,
Clement Read, Sen'r,
Thomas Bouldin,
Annas Carrell,
Jas. Boggs,
Henry Prewit,
Josiah Randle,
Henry Carver,
Geo. Lumkin,
Sarah Farmer,
Sherwood Walton,
Joshua Whorton,
Joshua Mullings,
Wm. Tooms, Jun'r,
Thomas Word,
Samuel Comer,
Robt. Saxton,
James Pettygrew,
Thomas Portwood,
Jas. Colwell,
Elizabeth Colwell,
Jas. Swillevant,
Paul Carrington,
John Haley,
Joshua Chafin,
John Cook,
Robert Davis,
David Craddock,
Wm. Goode,
Richard Hix, Sen'r,
Robert Breedlove,
James Spradlin,

49

Joseph Williams,
Joseph Akin,
Abraham Vaughan,
Gabriel Toombs,
David Winipey,
John Francis,
John Norrice,
John Blackwell,
Argal Blackston,
Barnard Wells,
Thomas Smith,
Sylvanah Stokes,
Elizabeth Stone,
Edward Slaughter,
Henry Hudson,
George Mosley,
Wm. Silcock,
Wm. Gilliam,
John Elmore,
Wm. Addams,
Abr'n Martin,
Francis Howard,
Jas. Murphy,
John Waller,
Benjamin Watson,
John Mason,

John Weatherfood,
Jos. Coleson,
William Coplin,
Thos. McCormack,
John Colwell,
Jas. Taylor,
Henry Coles,
John Cunningham,
Geo. Jones,
Geo. Anderson,
John Silcock,
Saml. Johnston,
Richard Jones,
John Agar,
Wm. Conner,
Elizabeth Roblet,
John Sansom,
Thomas Mitchell,
Michal Gill,
John William,
William Gill,
Jeremiah Childra,
Mary Jones,
Clement Read, Jun'r.
Charles Couples,
Wm. Jameson.

I have dug up, as it were, the names of individuals who lived long ago. They were honored in their generation, and were the glory of their times. "There be some of them that have left a name behind them that their praises might be reported. And some there be who have no memorial; who are perished as though they had never been born."

50

Sad reflection to some who long to "live in songs of distant days." But why should a mortal care for fame on this earth, if he believes that when he dies he will assume a new body, and career in a new and brighter world?

Now, gentle reader, I want to take your mind off the old account book, to give you a pen picture of my old aunt Mary Bouldin.

Twenty-four years ago I sat by a blazing fire of a winter's night, in company with several friends, listening to her while she was telling us the tales which I have told to you. She was then upwards of ninety years of age; but her head was clear, her spirits unbroken and she was as straight as an arrow.

She first touched upon Col. Clement Read, his landing at Williamsburg when a lad; his education at William and Mary college; his settlement afterward in Charlotte; his polished manners, high character and valuable services to Church and State. Then she gave us her early impression of "Madam Read," who, she said, was educated in all that was useful as well as ornamental. Her stately bearing; her strong family pride; her splendid furniture: the beautiful gravel walks and flowers and tall pyramids of cedars in her yard. Then she gave us a graphic account of Col. Thomas Bouldin, the most active, stirring man in the county, of his day; who built churches; carried on merchandise and farming; tamed "new negroes," and assisted in driving back the Indians.

Again she reverted to "Madam Read" whose character amused her exceedingly. She told us how that spirited old dame used to ride out in the plantation, giving orders to her hundred slaves: how, on one occasion, she bolted up stairs with a cowhide in hand and ran one of her sons out of the window; how she threatened to whip another for going to the mountains and getting married by a magis-

trate; how she speedily sent for Parson Johnston and had them married over according to the established usages of the Church. She then portrayed this zealous supporter of the establishment, dressed in lute-string silk, lawn apron and round top hat, as she walked majestically up the aisle, the eyes of the whole congregation upon her and took her seat in the upper pew, her silver can of water by her side.

Next she gave us a vivid picture of old Parson Johnston reading his sermon, while the dissenters were impatiently waiting for him to conclude in order that they might begin.

Then came a description of the amusements of the people in colonial days; their horse-racing; their card-playing; their shooting matches and their merry Christ-mases. The scenes of her childhood come up before her; she forgets that she is old; springs upon the floor, and, at the same time she mimics an old beau, she shows us how she used to dance the minuet. All enjoy the scene and each in his turn, asks a thousand questions. The old lady's heart lightens as she goes; she makes a hundred sprightly remarks; laughs at her own pictures; herself, the livliest picture of them all.

But presently the scene changes, some one advances a sentiment which displeases her. "It is not so, sir," says she, as she stamps her foot upon the floor; shakes her fist at him and "crows defiance in his face." The old lady is now on a high horse, and all herself appears in this one night's view.

We will now inform the reader that we have gone through the Old Trunk; that is to say, the papers which relate to colonial days. We have examined the original documents with great interest, but they must lose much of their magical effect when transferred to the pages of a

book. The old man who disguises the emblems of age; puts in a new set of teeth; dyes his hair and dresses in the height of fashion, is an old man nevertheless, but he loses half the charm which belongs to years. So these old papers, with the mellowness of age upon them, so suggestive in manuscript form, are robbed of much of their attractiveness when clothed in modern type. Still, they and the traditions connected with them are valuable mementoes of the past. They aid the memory in bringing back things long forgotten, calling up visions of scenes and forms of long ago and furnish us with pleasing contrasts, between the present and the past.

As we rummage over the Old Trunk of our forefather, containing papers of every description ; autographs of old pioneers, commissions of officers, signed by the ancient colonial Governors of Virginia, letters patent granted by George the Second, orders to march to the relief of the frontier, letters from a commission merchant in Glasgow to a planter in Lunenburg, an order upon the Collector of Cornwall Parrish to pay for the building of a church in 1769, an advertisement to let to the lowest bidder the poor people of the parrish, marriage licenses which were obtained when our grandmother was led to the hymeneal altar according to the ceremonies of the Church of England, levies by the county court for the purchase of arms for the poor, old account-books furnishing interesting hints of the private life of our forefathers, we say, as we rummage over this confused mass of papers belonging to an age when the laws, the manners and habits of the people were so different from what they are now, we go "stumbling o'er recollections," but they are not recollections of the pilgrim who stands amidst the ruins of Rome, "lone mother of dead empires," and plods "his way o'er steps of broken thrones and temples;" they remind us, not of

a people who have run their course, dazzling the eye for a while by their splendid career, whose cities were at length humbled, and its glories fled; but they remind us of the childhood of a mighty nation, the foundation of a magnificent structure, which in after years, reared its head to the heavens, the wonder and admiration of the civilized world; they impress the mind with the rapid strides which have been made within a few years towards the improvement of a country which our forefathers found a savage wild; they enlarge our views of the great changes which have taken place in our social fabric, and teach us what manner of people laid the foundation of this proud old Commonwealth.

ERRATA.

On the seventh page it is stated that Farley won 20,000 acres of Col. Byrd. It should be Col. Byrd's *son*.

On the eighth page, three lines from the bottom, for vietalizing read *rictualling*.

www.ingramcontent.com/pod-product-compliance
Lightning Source LLC
Chambersburg PA
CBHW060246030726

47493CB00025B/2723